Schools Council
Art and Craft Education 8–13 Project

USING OBJECTS

Visual Awareness and Visual Learning
in the Museum and Classroom

Schools Council
Art and Craft Education 8–13 Project

The project was set up to investigate art education and curriculum development for the 8–13 age group. It set out to make known and co-ordinate advances in art and craft teaching, bridging the gap particularly between primary and secondary schools, and to re-examine the contribution which art and the crafts, as an autonomous study, can make to children's development and how they can assist in the establishment of a flexible school curriculum. The main objective of the project team was to determine the nature of children's creative experience and to reach a finer understanding of the conditions which encourage their creative and imaginative growth.

MATERIALS PRODUCED

HANDBOOK

Children's Growth through Creative Experience
Art and Craft Education 8–13
This handbook is intended not only for teachers but for all those concerned with the education of children within the age-range of 8–13. It includes the findings of the Research Officers' detailed observation of children and teachers in schools, and of the conditions which favour or hinder creative work.

SOURCEBOOKS

Using Natural Materials by Seonaid Robertson
Using Constructional Materials by Michael Laxton
Using Objects by Renée Marcousé

Three supporting booklets which explore in depth suggestions and ideas for teachers in relation to the three sources, which are indicated in their titles.

DISCUSSION MATERIALS

These eleven sets of discussion material are in the form of half-frame film-strips with taped commentary. These are for use by groups of teachers in Teachers' Centres, in Colleges of Education, or elsewhere.

This discussion material is not intended to direct teachers or students to any pre-determined line of development in their work, but to promote debate on the values and purposes behind art and craft education.

THE TITLES	AREA OF WORK
Metropolis	Construction
Imagining with Clay	Clay work
Personal Adornment	Craft
Art in Transfer	Study of art/craft work
From Pleasure They Create	Museum studies
Messing about or Achieving Control?	Painting
Resistant Materials	Craft
What Have We Learnt?	Construction
Fantasy	Construction
Waste Materials	2- and 3-dimensional work
Whose Objectives?	Painting

Schools Council
Art and Craft Education 8–13 Project

Dr. Renée Marcousé
USING OBJECTS
Visual Awareness and Visual Learning
in the Museum and Classroom

VNR VAN NOSTRAND REINHOLD COMPANY
New York · Cincinnati · Toronto · London · Melbourne

Acknowledgements

I should like to thank the Curator and Staff of the Pitt Rivers Museum, Oxford for their help and co-operation and Mrs. Anne Robinson who worked with me in the pilot study.

Van Nostrand Reinhold Company Regional Offices:
New York   Cincinnati   Chicago   Millbrae   Dallas

Van Nostrand Reinhold Company International Offices:
London   Toronto   Melbourne

This book is set in Optima and is printed in
Great Britain by Jolly and Barber Ltd., Rugby, Warwickshire.

Published by Van Nostrand Reinhold Company Ltd.,
25–28 Buckingham Gate, London SW1E 6LQ, and
Van Nostrand Reinhold Company Inc., 450 West 33rd Street,
New York, N.Y. 10001.

16   15   14   13   12   11   10   9   8   7   6   5   4   3   2   1

Library of Congress Cataloging in Publication Data

Marcousé, Renée.
Using objects.
Includes bibliographical references.
1. Visual perception.   2. Visual education.
I. Title.
N7430.5.M29   701   74-4036
ISBN 0-442-30022-0

Visual Awareness
and
Visual Learning
in the
Museum

How we look, what we see, how we react to the same object is intensely varied and personal. Factual, objective information such as length, height, width, names, dates is accepted without query, but our response to the subjective element in ideas or colour, in shape or texture is personal and individual and is influenced by our associations and previous experiences. This personal response is inherent in visual awareness. It has to be recognized and carefully nurtured for it contains the germ of original creative thought and expression. It is my concern here to call attention to its visual potential as it relates to art, and to consider how such awareness can be developed in the child of middle school age.

The study of perception has long attracted the attention of the philosopher, the psychologist and those interested in aesthetics, and, more recently, art historians, such as Professor Arnheim and Sir Ernst Gombrich have stressed the contribution of visual learning in the study of art history. Today, questions relating to visual awareness, visual thinking, and perception, concern the layman as well as the specialist; there is more general appreciation that 'seeing' present difficulties, that all too often we are unaware of what we are looking at.

However, although visual awareness is now an accepted aim in art education and its significance in the aesthetic growth of the child generally recognized, little attempt is made to promote this actively in the classroom. Professor Arnheim in his book *Visual Thinking*[1] reproaches present day educational practices as being too biased towards verbal abstractions and points out that "visual form is not recognized as a medium of productive thinking". This may be partly due to present day emphasis on the new techniques and skills which figure so largely in art and craft teaching, but more probably to teachers' lack of experience in matters of perception.

In primary teaching, visual and verbal methods are better resolved than for the older age groups. Ten year-olds still see in visual terms; they have been encouraged to relate objects and image to verbal concepts. These children have experience of looking at interesting things in the school and in the environment; they know visual enjoyment; they are used to talking about things; they have looked at and heard visually exciting material freely discussed by other children and by adults. This often contrasts forcibly with the approach in the first years of secondary school where verbal concepts and abstractions take over with little reference to these earlier methods of visual learning.

[1] Arnheim, R. *Visual Thinking*. Faber and Faber, 1970.

Fig. 1. *Ceramic Plate*. Pablo Picasso. Private Collection.

Those who know the work of Picasso will recognize the signature of his style but what will appeal in this plate with its low relief and subdued colour tone to the 10 or 12 year-old? Will the seated figure of Pan playing his pipe strike a familiar chord and engage his eye? Will the waterside scene be sufficiently familiar? Will he recognize the cicada (Fig. 2) so typical of southern Europe? Will his previous associations and experience suffice, or how do we keep the eye engaged so that "The details become familiar, are read by the eye, filled in, re-angled in order to make sense, and the image becomes meaningful on his terms?"

A 13 year-old said: "I like it because it is all so spikey; bones like a skeleton and staring eyes squinting out of his head and spikey grass." He had never heard of Pan but recognized the pipe as a recorder and said it must be evening because the sun was setting. He did not at first see the cicada and then thought it was a grasshopper or a tadpole, which he pointed out would be found near water.

Fig. 2. Detail of *Ceramic Plate*.

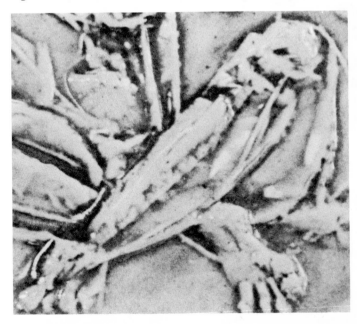

9

Fig. 3. *Wine Vessel in the form of a Short-Eared Owl. Bronze. Chinese 10–11th century B.C. Victoria and Albert Museum, Crown Copyright.*

It is on account of their special needs and difficulties in matters of visual awareness that this age group 11 to 13 is my particular concern here, and that the illustrations and examples relate to them. The discussion set *From Pleasure They Create*[1] which is an extension of this book covers the work of both younger and older age groups. Delight in objects which is characteristic of primary age groups does not disappear over-night unless thwarted and ignored. This eagerness to see is fertile ground which should be further cultivated so that thought indeed becomes active sight. If, for example, the 12 year-old learns visually to read an object and to relate it to his experience, to his overall pattern of understanding then 'seeing' becomes meaningful in terms of ideas. For "sight is active exploration rather than passive recording and is highly selective in concentrating on what attracts the attention".[2]

A group of 12 year-old girls hover in front of this bronze. They listen while the teacher reads the label; "Wine Vessel in the form of a Short-Eared Owl. Chinese, 10–11th century B.C." This appears to convey nothing and they look with even greater uncertainty. Suddenly one says: "It doesn't look like an owl. It is an old man with a beak-like nose wearing old-fashioned clothes with his hands behind his back." "No, it is a bird, look at the feathers" pointing to the inlay pattern barely visible on the wings and parts of the vessel. "Birds have claws," says a third, "and old men don't have beaks, and this one is curved and pointed like a bird's." "Yes, and the label says 'owl'." The label is read again, but this time they ask, "What is a wine vessel?" "Why is it made like this?" The teacher in turn asks, "Could it be for a special occasion? Does your Mother have things she uses at Christmas or for birthday parties?" Slowly this unfamiliar object begins to relate to their understanding; they look at it critically as if for the first time seeing it in terms of their experience of something with which they are familiar. They decided it looks 'cheeky'; 'perky'; 'amused'; "Are all Chinese animals like this?" The teacher tries to place the date for them; "What," she asks, "was happening in 1000 B.C. in this country? Ice Age? Iron Age? How were we living? Did this bronze and other things from the same period give some idea how the Chinese were living then? Were they in fact making things at that time similar to those we make today?" She then asks them to look for other animals in the same gallery, in the paintings, in clay, in bronze, in jade, to find out for themselves what the Chinese thought about animals. They now have a guide line and a point of departure. Without mentioning aesthetics or using terms which are incomprehensible, this teacher points the way for these children to a personal awareness of the quality of Chinese objects.

[1] Schools Council Art and Craft Education 8–13 Project. Discussion Set. *From Pleasure They Create.* Van Nostrand Reinhold, 1974.
[2] Arnheim, R. *Visual Thinking.* Faber and Faber, 1970.

Fig. 4. *Lion.* Grey-white porcelain. Chinese 10–11th century A.D. Victoria and Albert Museum. Crown Copyright.

Most people think of a lion as a fearsome creature but what will children say to this friendly beast, negligently scratching its ear? Will it remind them of their pets? Their cat? This is a grey lion: Does it matter? What does it tell us about the potter who made it?

Fig. 5. *Game of Polo* (Detail). Watercolour on Silk.
Chinese. Based on original 1280–1368. Lilin, active
1835. Victoria and Albert Museum, Crown Copyright.

*There is so much to catch the eye – the verve and
animation of rider and horse – the unexpected
postures as they twist and bend to reach the quoit –
the unfamiliar dress, with flat cap tied closely to the
head – skirt hitched up for convenience, long riding
boot and familiar stirrup. If asked to describe the
colours used by the artist, will there for some be
sudden consciousness of these delicate, infinitely
subtle blue-green tones with skilful use of red on
harness tassel and saddle cloth? And will the expert
amongst them explain to the less informed,
differences such as the long mane, the knotted tail,
the rounded saddle?*

14

Plate 2.   Egg-Shaped Agate. Indian. Private Collection. (See page 27.)

Fig. 6. *Buffalo.* Jade. Chinese 17th century A.D.
Victoria and Albert Museum, Crown Copyright.

*Who has seen a real buffalo? Was it like this? Placid
yet so alive? Friendly, ruminating, wholly at ease, he
has instant appeal. Is it the texture of jade with its
marbled effects, its coolness and smoothness which
make one want to feel it? Do the children know that
to the Chinese, jade was not only precious it was
almost holy? That its many tones of colour inspired
the potter's glaze? Dim white, deep green, its
hardness and fine grain, its toughness and durability,
the musical note it gives when struck. Awareness of
its many varieties, of its delicacy of colour and
texture deepen our understanding of ancient Chinese
thought and way of life.*

Plate 3.   Shell from Crete. Private Collection. (See page 30.)

Plate 4. Opposite.   Bronze Bird with Gold Inlay. Persian 18th century A.D. Private Collection. (See pages 42, 43.)

19

Fig. 7. *Horse's Head.* Earthenware. Chinese 8–9th century A.D. Victoria and Albert Museum. Crown Copyright.

Riding and experience of horses is becoming widespread amongst children and many can look at a head such as this on their own terms. This horse could be the point of contact which keeps the eye 'engaged' and allows for its quality of texture and colour to take effect. The experience may not be immediate; much will depend on the teacher's visual awareness if it is to lead to an effective learning situation.

Fig. 8. *Horse's Head from the Parthenon.* Greek 442 B.C. British Museum.

"Perception helps talking and talking fixes the grains of perception."[1]

Where a child is familiar with this visual process of looking, discussing, comparing an object of today with an object from Greece or from China, he learns to apprehend differences as well as similarities. If a teacher is alerted to the advantages of studying a particular theme such as 'horses' and other animals in different civilizations, the child has a 'guide line' to enable him to make his own discoveries, his own deductions which he should later be encouraged to share with the teacher and his classmates. The process of sharing is indeed a vital part of visual learning.

[1] Gibson, James J. *The Senses Considered as Perceptual Systems.* Allen & Unwin, 1948.

22

Plate 6.　Children's Objects in the Classroom. (See page 48.)

Plate 5. Opposite.　Ceramic Tile. Lurcin. French 1958. Private
Collection. (See page 44.)

Fig. 9. *Embroidery*. English 16th Century A.D.
Victoria and Albert Museum, Crown Copyright.

*Animals known and unknown in a setting of trees
and flowers, familiar and unfamiliar which were
found in Elizabethan England. How many are still
found in the countryside today?*

All too often those entering secondary school take refuge in the conventional group attitude. New surroundings, other traditions, academic subjects, adolescent problems all tend to diminish personal confidence and to make the group viewpoint more desirable and acceptable. Individual response with its creative potential will often vanish under these pressures unless consciously encouraged and nurtured by the teacher. It is his responsibility to recognize the special needs of this age group and to appreciate the extent to which such awareness develops sensibility and stimulates the imagination.

Experience shows that visual awareness develops in unexpected ways, that it may be the aesthetic quality of form, colour, texture and content which arrest the eye and quicken response. These are of the essence of the visual experience but what do we understand by them, how do we awaken them in child or adult so that the mind is stimulated to fresh understanding of things seen?

Museums of all kinds provide an ideal introduction to visual thinking and visual learning. In an art museum, there is great wealth and variety of objects. Though not always understood in their correct context they evoke our imagery. Some have the quality of rarity only to be found in great collections, others, familiar things, but seen in a different setting, acquire new qualities, new significance. By means of such contrasts, the eye is alerted to new concepts.

Today school visits to museums are officially encouraged and efforts are being made to discover new ways to use the museum as an active learning medium.[1] At one time the introductory talk or lecture was popular but it is now realized that if information is given too forcibly by the well-informed teacher, a barrier can be set up, which hinders the child from seeing the object for himself and from forming his own impressions. It is undoubtedly part of our task as educators to make known what others have thought and created at other times, and to provide the historical, objective framework. But the child's confidence in his barely formulated visual image, can all too easily be shattered if subjected to a battery of unknown facts; to become meaningful these facts must relate to the child's experience and to what the object conveys to his eye.

[1] Schools Council: *Pterodactyls and Old Lace: Museums in Education*. Evans/Methuen Educational, 1972.

Fig. 10. *Egg-Shaped Agate*. Indian. Private Collection.

To one child this agate will appeal because of the variety of colour tones; to another it will be the smoothness; to a third the oval shape which curves to the hand will stir his visual imagery. Is the teacher aware how greatly this experience varies from child to child and of its significance? It is this personal experience that has potential learning value.

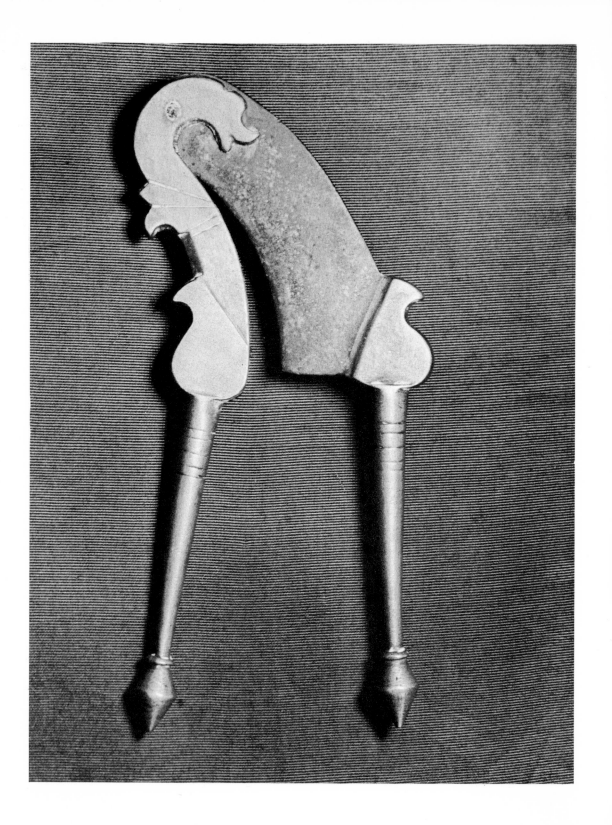

Fig. 12. *Betel Nutcracker.* Detail.

Fig. 11. Opposite.
Betel Nutcracker in the form of a Bird.
Brass. Indian 19th century A.D. Private Collection.

This could lead to unexpected insight into the Indian way of life. The point of contact for one may be the knife; for another the bird form which recalls the stork; and what further questions will it rouse when its use is understood – the crushing of the Betel nut? Will it help them to appreciate what this nut means to the Indian if it is likened to the role chewing gum still plays in the West?

Figs. 13–15.   *Shell from Crete.* Private Collection.

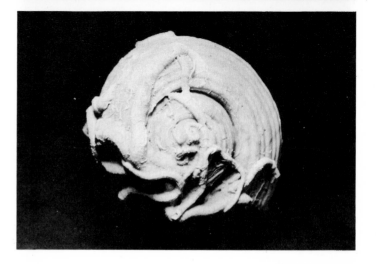

"How to describe shape and colour?"

"When I hold it and shut my eyes, it feels rough, jagged and then smooth; there are ridges like mountains but they feel round; if you follow them with your finger, they disappear and the surface is scratchy. There are lots of ridges at one end but the other is open and curved and deeper at one side. I feel inside, my fingers echo and make a noise like the sea. When I hold it close to my ear there is the same sound, very far away, just an echo. No, I have never heard of Crete. Yes, I would like to write about this shell and the sea. At first I thought it had no colour but now it makes me think of cream with ridges a deeper colour the way cream turns after it is open some time. And other parts shine and look transparent grey-black like my dog's toe nails. Was it the water that made it so smooth and shiny? And how did these bits grow on top? I like to hold it so that I see the sandy ridges inside – it's not real sand but looks like it – and above, the ridges are like worms crawling as if trying to get inside." (Boy of 11 plus.)

Other children had different impressions; one saw it as a sea urchin; another was solely concerned with the ribbed lines but to all it recalled personal associations of the sea.

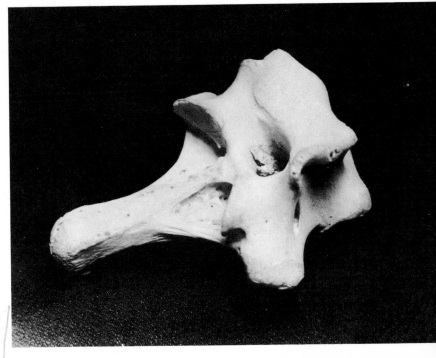

Response is important in any teaching situation for it implies personal reaction and individual involvement with ideas as with objects. To encourage a child to have confidence in his personal image or viewpoint is a first step in training him to look, to discuss, to relate and to understand. As James J. Gibson says: "Perception helps talking and talking fixes the grains of perception."[1]

It is enlightening for child as for teacher to discover how various these responses are; on what objects different eyes linger with the most pleasure; the colouring of the agate, the evocative shape of the bronze wine vessel in the shape of an owl or what Manley Hopkins calls the 'delicate inscape' of a bone structure or the strange formation and texture of a shell. What is it that appeals to one child and is abhorrent to another? Shape or colour tones? How to describe these shapes and colours? How to convince the inexperienced child or adult that there is no one criterion of right or wrong in this matter of choice? That he has the right to prefer the Great Sword to the Chinese Bowl, that he has the right to change his mind if his first pleasure and interest lessen when he becomes more familiar with it. How to overcome the diffidence of:

"Because I don't know what it is, I can't look at it."

It takes time and practice to read an object visually, to relate to it and to learn more about it.

Fig. 16.   *Bone Structure.* Skeleton of Bird's Beak. Private Collection.
   "To discover what is curious, strange, to give effect to creative expression in another form."[2]

[1] Gibson, James J. *The Senses Considered as Perceptual Systems.* Allen & Unwin, 1968.

[2] Schools Council Art and Craft Education 8 to 13 Project. Discussion Set. *From Pleasure They Create.* Van Nostrand Reinhold, 1974.

Figs. 17–19. Above; Opposite, above and below.
"The use of the pencil to keep the child longer in the presence." Copyright, Pitt Rivers Museum, Oxford.

In the museum, this engagement with the object can be achieved in various ways, by asking the student to select something he likes, to note by word or sketch a detail which is specially pleasing and which will later help him to recall his pleasure. Selection is valuable for it calls for both effort and commitment. It leads to personal awareness of likes and dislikes which are all too easily ignored. The selection, moreover, of a particular detail of a particular object implies that it appeals more to the imagination, to the interest of the individual concerned. It relates to his personal response and is therefore more meaningful to him than any details selected by the teacher. The latter is usually all too willingly adopted for it requires much less effort than personal selection.

Sketching is a valuable part of this training in sensibility and visual awareness. It not only keeps the eye engaged but is an excellent starting point in deciphering an unfamiliar object visually. This use of the pencil to make notes is not intended as with art students, to teach drawing, perspective or skilled copying thereby distracting attention and diminishing immediacy in appreciation of the object. Its purpose is to hold the child longer in the presence, to make him look more attentively and allow time to relate what he is told or knows to what he sees, so that image and concept together promote new ideas and lead to greater understanding.

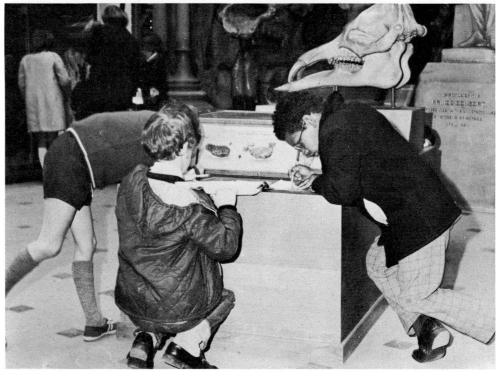

Figs. 20–21. Left and below.
"The eye engaged." Copyright, Pitt Rivers Museum, Oxford.

Fig. 22. Opposite.
"To look more attentively." Photograph, Henry Grant.

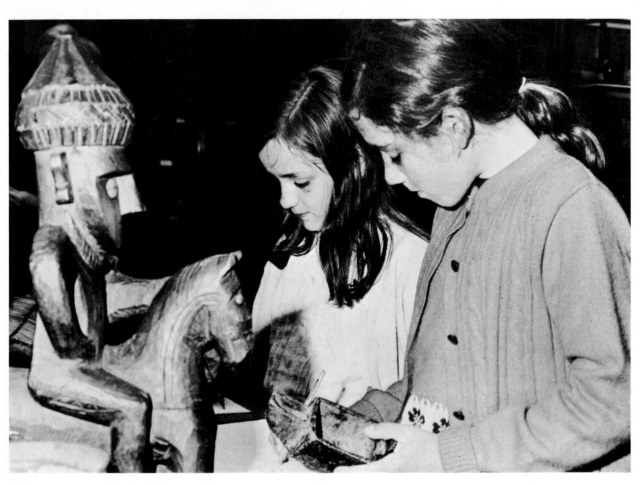

Fig. 23.
Greater awareness, greater understanding can also be realised by movement. Photograph J. P. B. Verheij Pols.

Fig. 24.
Verbal comment is by no means excluded; it is a matter of knowing how and when to make known what others have created at other times, so as to increase understanding and encourage individual response. Sometimes the tape recorder provides the information required. When the child finds the verbal content too indigestible and not sufficiently related to the object, he stops listening. Photograph, Henry Grant.

It is constructive for children to compare their choice with that of their peers. Seeing through another child's eyes and learning about his reactions leads to fresh insights about objects which had been looked at from another point of view. Such discussion if begun in the museum should continue in the classroom where visual memory will be helped by the child's notes and sketches. Details seen by one may in all probability have been ignored by another, until recalled by a description or drawing.

Fig. 25. Left. *Bronze Handle Attachment from the Aylesford Bucket*. Celtic 1 B.C. British Museum.

Asked to describe this mask-like head, one was struck by the prominent headgear, another by the protruding eyes, the tight-lipped mouth. When asked to compare this with objects of other periods, they begin to recognize the characteristic linearity of Celtic ornament.

Fig. 26. Opposite. *Bronze Door-knocker*. Durham Cathedral 11th century A.D.

How does this door-knocker of Viking origin compare with the earlier Celtic design? What effect did the artist wish to give? Forbidding rather than welcoming? Protection for those within from the Viking invader? Distortion more deliberate or realistic than in the Celtic head?

"Personal choice is more meaningful than any object selected by the teacher."

This sculpture roused much interest when shown to a class of 12 year-olds. For the majority, it was their first contact with modern sculpture and they were responsive to its abstract quality. They had no difficulty in comparing this with Figs. 29 and 31 in terms of a visual exercise in contrasting styles. They were then asked to assess the object in terms of its period.

Fig. 27. *Bird-man.* Contemporary Iron Sculpture. Private Collection.

Fig. 28. *Bird-man*. Detail

"I call this 'Road Runner', a bird shown in a cartoon series on T.V. This one is made by an artist living today. . . . I like the feel of it and the noise it makes when I tap it. It is very heavy – the bark of a tree, dented, sharp and rough." (Comment of girl 12 plus.)

Fig. 29. *Bronze Bird with Gold Inlay.* Persian 18th century A.D. Private Collection.

"The curve of the neck and head looks proud, haughty – the comb stiff, beak curved ready to peck – cruel. Legs like matchsticks with feet touching to give it balance. These are not real birds' claws but what one might think a bird's claw should be. I like the flecks of gold and silver which mark the feathers on the wings and neck. Its tail is curved and scalloped but stands upright; if I had this I would fill its tail with flowers." (Girl of 12.)

She later made a painting of a bird with a profusion of flowers in place of his tail.

Fig. 30. *Bronze Bird*. Rear view.

Fig. 32. Opposite.   *Responses in Clay*. Photograph, Henry Grant.

There are many facets to learning and this insistence on visual response by no means excludes verbal explanation. The aim is to develop a learning situation in which the visual potential is fully utilized. Lord Clark gives an enlightening description of the interplay of visual and verbal experience in his book *Looking at Pictures*. He points out that looking requires active participation and in the early stages, a certain amount of discipline. "On the whole, I have found my feelings fall into the same pattern of impact, scrutiny, recollection and renewal. . . . In the middle of the exercise, my senses begin to tire and if I am to go on looking responsively, I must fortify myself with nips of information. One cannot enjoy the smell of an orange for very long, which in my case, is less than two minutes; but one must look attentively at a great work of art for longer than that. . . . As I remember the facts of a painter's life and try to fit the picture in front of me into its place in his development, my powers of receptivity are gradually renewing themselves and suddenly make me aware of a beautiful passage of drawing or colour which I should have overlooked, had not an intellectual pretext kept my eye unconsciously engaged."[1]

It is for the teacher to provide the 12 year-old with the equivalent of these 'nips of information', to evoke ways such as these already mentioned to keep the mind alert and eye engaged so that the child can look responsively. And it is only when the teacher has experienced the difficulties and pleasures inherent in visual learning that he appreciates how spontaneously visual impact can spark off original creative reaction in art as in the other disciplines.

[1] Clark, Sir Kenneth. *Looking at Pictures*. John Murray, 1960.

Fig. 31. Below.   *Ceramic Tile*. Lurcin. French 1958. Private Collection.

How does this compare with the Persian cock in bronze? One is free standing and the other is in low relief, have they anything in common? Is one more cock-like? How does each achieve its effect? Line? Colour? Movement? This type of question does not call for specialist information; the answers are to be found in the object, by close observation, deduction and visual awareness. It is astonishingly difficult to persuade students of all ages that if they look at the object, they will find the answers and that "they don't have to know about it before they look at it".

44

Visual Awareness
and
Visual Learning
in the
Classroom

Museums with their exciting visual displays are an obvious source of visual learning. They stimulate the eye and incite endless questions as the child responds to what he sees and tries to relate this to his understanding. It is in the museum that the teacher learns to appreciate the extent to which personal ideas and imagery are incited both visually and verbally; how the evocative statement can increase visual awareness of the external world. All too often this visual contribution is overlooked, if not destroyed by an over-emphatic factual approach, for it is no easy matter to make mind and eye equally receptive.

Of necessity, much depends on the attitude of the teacher and on his personal response to visual learning with objects. Much also depends on prevailing methods of teaching. Children accustomed to inter-disciplinary methods respond more quickly than those taught by a formal, academic approach. The former expects individual exploration and enquiry; it encourages individual thought; personal opinion and perceptive, visual learning are integral to the process. On the other hand, there is often suspicion and resistance on the part of children if attempts are made to instigate individual response with

Fig. 33. *Unpacking the objects.*

special emphasis on the visual approach at the expense of more traditional methods of teaching.

It might be helpful to point some of the difficulties experienced in this respect in a country-based secondary school when trying out a learning situation with objects. Any young, enthusiastic teacher imbued with current ideas on visual learning might be faced with a similar situation and it is no easy matter to break down the group resistance of 12 year-old girls accustomed to formal classroom methods.

In this school the art teacher was already committed to visual learning; she was anxious from the outset that this experience would be productive of visual imagery and stimulate individual creative work. She had the class for a two and a half hour period each week and the exercise in question lasted six weeks.

The work was object-based. It included visits to the museum but began in the classroom with a miscellaneous collection brought it both by the teacher and by the children. The teacher's choice was varied and ranged from a basket-woven carpet beater to an Indian brass foot-scraper, from a Chinese bronze rat to natural objects

such as a shell or lilyhead. These were unpacked by the girls in the art room and put on long tables, each with a simple label saying what it was, where it came from. There was general excitement as the class looked and handled but involvement was not immediate. (See Figs 33–4.)

It is often assumed handling is sufficient in itself to stimulate response. Such involvement does occur if the student can relate the object to his personal experience. If he can fill it in or re-angle it so that it makes sense. Otherwise, he requires help in tactile learning, similar to that required in visual learning. Faced with many unfamiliar things put there for him to handle, the child is all too apt just to lift object after object, look at it for a few minutes and replace it often without comment or question. Unable to make contact, he is at a loss what to see, to say or to think. In this instance, however, the class was asked to discover which objects were pleasing to touch; what was heavy, or cool or smooth? They disagreed; they argued and began to show some awareness of what they held. They made notes, sketched and later sketched again from memory. Some, blindfolded, discovered that they could not identify the things

47

Fig. 34.   *Handling and discussing the objects.*

Fig. 35.   *Objects from home.*

they had handled because they had not been visually meaningful. For these children tactile impressions lead to more positive visual identification.

The class were willing and eager to co-operate in this visual venture but the method of work was wholly unfamiliar and their first responses were commonplace and conventional. There was no spark of personal pleasure, no violent likes or dislikes; no starting points for further discussion. They reacted as one group apparently unwilling, perhaps unable, to make individual comment. To find out if they would react differently to their own objects they were asked to bring one or two things they liked from home in the hope that this might induce a more personal attitude. Their choice was revealing of their limited background and lack of interests; it consisted for the most part of toys – plastic or cloth animals and gnomes. (See Fig. 35.) These were childhood symbols to which they were very attached. Although it was stressed that no one sees the same thing in the same way, that there is no question of right or wrong in the matter of personal preference, the group failed to come to terms with the objects and had difficulty in committing themselves to the choice of one particular object.

In a final attempt to break down this group resistance, it was proposed that each write a 'nonsense' story about a particular object, beginning with the words "I dreamt that".

This gambit opened the way to personal statements and they ceased to react as a group. If a story was 'nonsense', no one would judge it; they could say what they liked without fear of ridicule or of transgressing the code of group behaviour. They wrote without hesitation, imaginatively, quite unlike their previous uncertain jottings. Each was willing and eager moreover to read her story aloud.

They then illustrated their stories and this individual approach carried over into their paintings which had the same perceptive and personal quality in direct contrast to their first efforts.

Figs. 36, 37. *The Woolly Toy* and first painting of it.

The Woolly Toy Story:
   "*I dreamt an extraordinary thing happened. On a planet in the sea I saw a peculiar object. He had star eyes and a white beard and spoke with a Scottish accent, he had flabby feet and swam with these to aid him. I went to his hole, a big smelly thing and I saw his mother, daughter and uncle. I flew down to earth; he followed me and became my toy, but he had fits and now and again he would stand on his head, turn round twenty times singing 'With rain drops dropping on my head'.*"

Fig. 38. *Illustration of the Woolly Toy Story.*

Fig. 39.   *The Owl and first painting of it.*

The Owl Story:
   "I was going to a football match to see Manchester United v. Manchester City. When City came on, there was only ten players. We all waited for a few minutes and then onto the field came an owl. It had a yellow stomach, an orange nose and blue eyes. Everybody burst out laughing. The match still went on with the owl playing and he scored all the goals. He could score because he was so small and he went through all the legs and he became footballer of the year."

Fig. 40.   *Illustration of the Owl Story.*

Fig. 41. *The Looby Whistle and first painting of it.*

Fig. 42. *Illustration of the Looby Whistle Story.*

The Looby Whistle Story:

"I dreamt of my Spanish Looby Whistle. His hat was as big as his face and his face was like a plant pot with ears sticking out. Arms like sticks and no legs, yet I thought it walked. The Whistle was as big as his arms. The top part of his body was like a sweet, with no paper on, the bottom half like a plastic pot but upside down. He even had something round his neck."

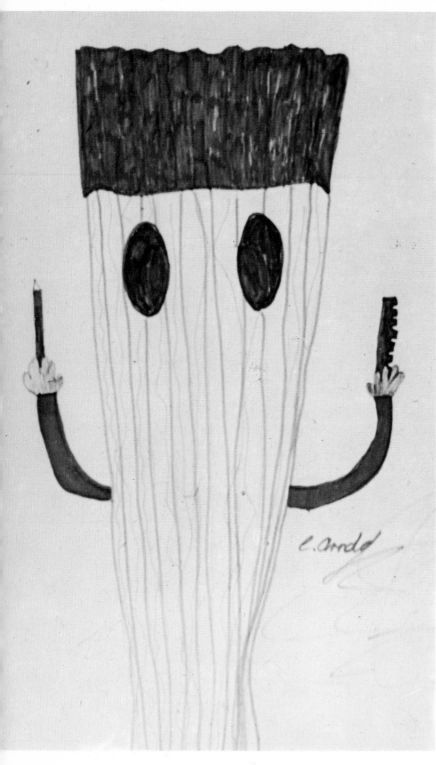

The Fan Story:
  "I dreamt about a fan, which was red and going round the room, blowing things down. It came over to my bed and thumped me. I got out of bed and kicked it. To my surprise it said, 'Shut up'. Then it went out of the room. It took with it a comb and a pencil. The fan used the pencil to comb its hair and used the comb to draw on the wall."

Fig. 43.   *Illustration of the Fan Story.*

The Plastic Gnome Story:
  "I dreamt I was in a room; it was dark but the light was shining in. I could see something moving. I could see white hair; it was coming closer and it looked very nasty but I could not see it very well for there was not too much light. I moved away but it came closer and closer. Now I could see a red pair of shorts and bloodshot eyes."

Fig. 44. Opposite.   *Illustration of the Plastic Gnome Story.*

These girls who had been silent and inarticulate in their first reactions to objects were now responding to visual and emotional stimulus. They were eager to express their ideas in their own terms. As Professor Arnheim puts it, "The more practised and nimble the mind becomes in scanning the rush inflow of information from pieces that fit together as in a jigsaw puzzle, the more skilled it is likely to become in productive thinking."[1] But this exercise was indeed only a beginning as far as the class was concerned and it required continuous effort on the part of the teacher to develop and strengthen their newly found freedom of expression, to encourage cross-fertilization into other disciplines.

The process was further implemented by a visit to the local museum. Two galleries were selected – the Egyptian room and the collections of live reptiles and fish. The class chose their objects and to encourage more intensive observations, made quick drawings or notes. These in turn led to divergent ideas set off by the object itself. Crocodile and snake were the most popular; the toad was a good runner-up.

Two weeks later, the class was asked to remember their feelings when they looked at these creatures. The teacher again pointed the way. She said: "Looking up, you see not the museum roof but the sky – there is the sun above – your feet move in wet sand – there is no longer any glass between you and the reptile. Now continue the story."

They had to be brief and use descriptive words; they wrote quickly, with considerable confidence. Their imagery was again very individual and in most cases, stimulated by fear.

[1] Arnheim, R. *Visual Thinking*. Faber and Faber, 1970.

The Snake Story:

"It was there right ahead of me, a snake, only a small snake, but it was growing larger and larger all the time, it kept growing until it was as big as a crocodile. It was coming nearer and nearer to me, I was edging my way back until I could go no further. The snake came so close that it touched me. Then I saw darkness and tumbling down and down until I was in its stomach. Everything I wanted was there: food, furniture, and water. Suddenly, the snake began to shrink again. I started to panic. I walked away from the room and jumped into a blood stream. I travelled all the way up. The snake was getting smaller and smaller, then I saw light. I came up into its mouth, then jumped out just in time. I saw the snake slowly shrink and wriggle back into the grass. I gave a sigh of relief and fell to the ground." (The snake is done with string and glue.)

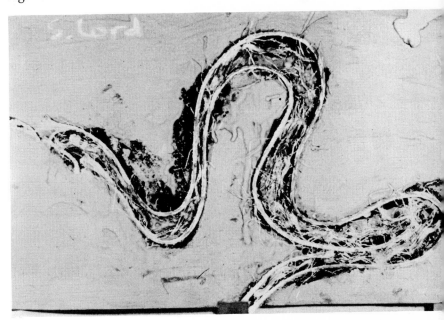

Fig. 45.   *Illustration of the Snake Story.*

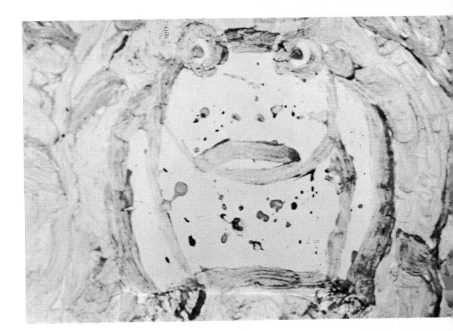

The Bull Frog Story:

"I stood petrified, its large mouth opened, its throat puffed out like a big bubble. The sun was blinding, the heat was tremendous, the bullfrog looked enormous. My heart began to beat quickly. The sweat ran off my head. I was lost in the jungle. I was frightened and even the smallest creature made me jump. The fat slimy green body made me shudder. All it had to do was to open its mouth and I would be gone. It jumped, I half fell and down I went. I woke up in bed."

Fig. 46.   *Illustration of the Bull Frog Story.*

The paintings done prior to writing have less fantasy. It is possible that the verbal tradition of learning in the school made it more natural for the pupils to express themselves creatively in words rather than in images though their initiation to visual thinking took place in the art room.

This study took six weeks to reach a point of dialogue between child and object – a personal imaginative dialogue in a world of fantasy. Increase in confidence and the easing of tension made this possible. It could with another teacher have developed in other ways; to the discovery for example of relationships in weight and measurements of reptiles, to climatic conditions relating to physical form. Such investigations would lead to experience in science, in mathematics, and to creativity in other disciplines.

We are surrounded at all times by objects which relate to new concepts, to visual and verbal imagery provided the eye is attuned to transmit the message. Thomas Traherne speaking of his own childhood says: "It was a difficult matter to persuade me that the tinselled ware upon a hobby-horse was a fine thing. . . . I could not see where was the curiousness or the fineness. Everyone," he complained, "provided objects; but few prepare senses whereby and light wherein, to see them."